by Myka-Lynne Sokoloff
illustrated by Johanna van der Sterre

Copyright © by Harcourt, Inc.

All rights reserved. No part of this publication may be reproduced or transmitted in any form or by any means, electronic or mechanical, including photocopy, recording, or any information storage and retrieval system, without permission in writing from the publisher.

Requests for permission to make copies of any part of the work should be addressed to School Permissions and Copyrights, Harcourt, Inc., 6277 Sea Harbor Drive, Orlando, Florida 32887–6777. Fax: 407-345-2418.

HARCOURT and the Harcourt Logo are trademarks of Harcourt, Inc., registered in the United States of America and/or other jurisdictions.

Printed in Mexico
ISBN 10: 0-15-350276-7
ISBN 13: 978-015-350276-7

Ordering Options
ISBN 10: 0-15-349940-0 (Grade 5 ELL Collection)
ISBN 13: 978-0-15-349940-1 (Grade 5 ELL Collection)
ISBN 10: 0-15-357311-2 (package of 5)
ISBN 13: 978-0-15-357311-8 (package of 5)

If you have received these materials as examination copies free of charge, Harcourt School Publishers retains title to the materials and they may not be resold. Resale of examination copies is strictly prohibited and is illegal.

Possession of this publication in print format does not entitle users to convert this publication, or any portion of it, into electronic format.

2 3 4 5 6 7 8 9 10   126   10 09 08 07

"I see him!" Miguel shouted. He pointed to a man with dark gray hair. The man walked out the door of his plane.

"He looks just like the picture," Javier added. "Papi, Mami, come quickly!"

Javier and Miguel had never met their mother's father. It was the first time Abuelo had visited the United States. The boys could not wait to hear stories about Puerto Rico.

Abuelo rested after the ride from the airport. The boys and Abuelo spoke together later that night. Javier said, "Abuelo, tell us about Puerto Rico. Tell us about when you were a boy."

"Children, I will tell you about my island," said Abuelo. "It is the land of my heart. The weather is mild. The beaches are very pretty. Summer lasts all year long. The flowers never sleep. Salsa music is everywhere. The people love to dance. The island is beautiful.

"Puerto Rico has changed much since I was a boy," Abuelo went on. "Today many people live in the city of San Juan. The city has tall buildings and fast cars. Tourists walk the stone streets of my childhood."

"Tell us more," said Javier.

"Puerto Rico seemed much smaller when I was a boy," said Abuelo. "Everybody knew everybody in my neighborhood. We had the same friends our whole lives."

Abuelo continued. "The best day of the year is still the Night of San Juan. It is at the end of June. The day is long. The night is short. In fact, it is the shortest night of the year. Each year we have a party."

"Why is this the best day for you, Abuelo?" Miguel asked.

"The Night of San Juan changed my life," Abuelo said. "I lived with my grandmother when I was a boy. She loved me very much. However, she worried about me all the time.

"She never let me play with the other children in the neighborhood. She was always afraid something would happen to me. I was very lonely. Summer was the hardest time because school was not in session."

"You mean you liked school better than summer?" the boys asked.

"Yes," said Abuelo. "In school, I played with my friend Evelyn and other boys and girls. We played ball at lunchtime. We chased each other around the school yard."

"Just like we do," interrupted Javier.

"*Shh*, let Abuelo tell the story," said Miguel.

Their grandfather continued. "In summer, my *abuela,* or grandmother, made me stay in the apartment most of the time. Now we did have some fun together. She taught me to cook and play games. She told me about when she was a little girl. Still, I watched the other kids from my balcony. I saw them eating ice cream and whispering together."

"Why didn't your grandmother let you play outdoors?" asked the boys.

"My *abuela* always worried. She worried about everything! She thought the street was a dangerous place. She was afraid of cars. She thought I would get hurt if I fell. Now I know she was just trying to protect me, but it really wasn't necessary.

"You see," he continued, "we lived in Old San Juan. Back then it was a small neighborhood. It was very safe. Everyone knew everyone's business. Children did not dare do anything wrong. Parents would know if children had done something wrong before the children arrived home!"

"Did you ever get into trouble, Abuelo?" asked Miguel.

"I never had the chance!" he said. "I just watched the other children from my balcony. I liked to watch Evelyn and her sisters on the street below. The littlest one was a real delight! She was so daring and mischievous. She was always trying something new. She always had a lot of fun!"

He smiled and said, "One time the girls wanted some ice cream. However, they had no money. They gathered some colored pencils and drew pictures of the island's landscape. They displayed the drawings on the street. The little one told people the prices for the drawings. In a little while, the girls had enough money to buy ice cream!"

"What did you do on the Night of San Juan?" Javier asked.

"People made big fires on the beach," Abuelo said. "They ate treats. Everyone walked backwards into the water. They jumped over the waves and made wishes. It was said that doing that would make bad things go away. I did not go to the beach. My grandmother worried too much."

"Then why do you like the Night of San Juan?" asked Miguel.

"One year, Evelyn and her sisters made a plan. They knew I was lonely. They wanted to help. They came to see my grandmother. The girls came up to my apartment. I was surprised when my grandmother invited them inside. It was the day of the Night of San Juan. Evelyn's family went to the beach each year, like many other people from Puerto Rico."

"Tell us more, Abuelo," said the boys.

"The girls asked my grandmother to let me go. I waited nervously while she made up her mind. She was reluctant at first. However, the girls were so nice and polite. At last, my *abuela* said I could go.

"We had a wonderful time. We all held hands and waded into the water backwards. We made wishes while we jumped over the waves."

"What did you wish, Abuelo?" Miguel asked his grandfather.

"I wished that I would always have good friends like Evelyn and her sisters. I wished that my grandmother would let me play with others more often. I wished that she would not worry so much," Abuelo answered.

"Did your wishes come true?" asked Javier.

"My wishes did come true! After that, my *abuela* let me play with the others. She decided she could trust my friends and me," said their grandfather.

"Did you stay friends with the girls?" the boys asked.

"Oh, yes," said Abeulo. "Didn't I tell you the name of Evelyn's littlest sister? It was Amalia."

"That was grandmother's name, too," Miguel said.

"Yes, it *was* your grandmother's name. In fact, she was your grandmother. You see, I married little Amalia when we both grew up!"

"Wow!" the boys cried. "Can we celebrate the Night of San Juan, too?"

"I would enjoy that," Abuelo responded, smiling. "However, there's no ocean here. We'll have to walk backwards into your pool."

The boys cheered.

Scaffolded Language Development

USING ADJECTIVES Remind students that an adjective is a word that describes a noun. Review these examples of adjectives from the story:

> He pointed to a man with dark gray hair. *(page 3)*
> The weather is mild. *(page 5)*

In the first sentence, *gray* describes the color of Abuelo's hair. In English, adjectives often come directly before a noun, as in this example. (Note: In many languages, such as Spanish and French, this order is often reversed. You may want to stress this difference to students in your class who speak these and/or other Romance languages.)

In the second sentence, *mild* describes the weather. Tell students, sometimes adjectives come after the verb.

Page through the story with students, finding other examples of adjectives. Help students identify the word each adjective describes.

🌏 Social Studies

Puerto Rico Fact File The Commonwealth of Puerto Rico is a territory of the United States. Have students locate Puerto Rico on a map and find out more about the island territory. Have them make a list of quick facts about Puerto Rico, including language, population, location, and so on.

School-Home Connection

Past Friendships Have students talk with family members about important friendships that they and their family members have.

Word Count: 1,068

Scaffolded Language Development

USING PROPER NOUNS Point out to students the words *Duke of Milan, Charlie Dent, Pennsylvania,* and *Italy.* Remind students that these words are proper nouns. Review proper nouns with students. The names of specific people and places are proper nouns. The names of holidays are also proper nouns. The main words in proper nouns always begin with capital letters. Explain that words like *of* do not count as main words—even in languages other than English!

Ask students to identify and capitalize the proper nouns in the following sentences:

1. lenoardo da vinci is my favorite painter. (Remember: *da* is another way of saying "of.")
2. charles dent lived in pennsylvania.
3. The french army marched into milan, italy.
4. The horse will be a symbol of friendship between america and italy.
5. Like da vinci, I want to be a famous artist.

🌐 Social Studies

What Else Happened? Have students choose one of the years that headlines each of the entries in Leonardo's journal. Tell them to research other events that occurred in the same year and take notes on what they discover.

School-Home Connection

Have students ask family members to name their favorite artists and discuss why they like the work of those artists.

Word Count: 903 (with graphic 907)